T0390253

LIFE CYCLES ON THE FARM

LIFE CYCLE OF A
HORSE

by Noah Leatherland

BEARPORT
PUBLISHING

Minneapolis, Minnesota

Credits

All images are courtesy of Shutterstock.com, unless otherwise specified. With thanks to Getty Images, Thinkstock Photo, and iStockphoto. Cover – Erik Lam, Semenaka_Maria. Recurring images – Mubeen Arif, uiliaaa, YummyBuum, tanyaya, Terdpong, Borodatch. 2 – Marie Charouzova, Erica Hollingshead. 4–5 – Dernkadel, violetblue, leungchopan, siro46, QBR, Q88, polkadot_photo. 6–7 – Callipso88, Annabell Gsoedl, vvvita. 8–9 – Marie Charouzova, pfluegler-photo. 10–11 – OryPhotography, Sozina Kseniia, purple_queue, Melissa E Dockstader. 12–13 – Kzerkel, Callipso88. 14–15 – Barry Fowler, Cynthia Kidwell. 16–17 – Callipso88, Conny Sjostrom. 18–19 – vprotastchik, Erica Hollingshead. 20–21 – Dhimas Satriaa, Kwadrat, Perpis, miroslav chytil, Pixel-Shot. 22–23 – Anastasija Popova, Naurider, Olga_i, LightField Studios.

Bearport Publishing Company Product Development Team

Publisher: Jen Jenson; Director of Product Development: Spencer Brinker; Managing Editor: Allison Juda; Editor: Cole Nelson; Associate Editor: Naomi Reich; Associate Editor: Tiana Tran; Designer: Kim Jones; Designer: Kayla Eggert; Designer: Steve Scheluchin; Production Specialist: Owen Hamlin

Library of Congress Cataloging-in-Publication Data is available at www.loc.gov or upon request from the publisher.

ISBN: 979-8-89577-016-0 (hardcover)
ISBN: 979-8-89577-447-2 (paperback)
ISBN: 979-8-89577-133-4 (ebook)

For more information, write to Bearport Publishing, 5357 Penn Avenue South, Minneapolis, MN 55419.

Contents

WHAT IS A LIFE CYCLE?

All living things go through different stages of life. We come into the world and grow over time. Eventually, we die. This is the life cycle.

BABY

TODDLER

CHILD

ADULT

TEENAGER

OLDER PERSON

As humans, we start life as babies. We grow into toddlers and children. Then, we become teenagers. Finally, we are adults and get even older. We may have babies of our own, and then the cycle begins again.

HORSES ON THE FARM

Animals on the farm go through life cycles, too. Farm horses are **domestic** animals. This means they are not wild. People keep them as **livestock**.

There are hundreds of different kinds of horses.

Many farms have only a few horses, while others may have more than 100. Farmers raise these animals to do jobs on the farm.

7

GETTING READY FOR FOALS

Adult **female** horses can have babies. Usually, a **pregnant** horse has only one baby, called a foal, growing inside her at a time. After about 11 months, the foal is ready to be born.

A PREGNANT HORSE

8

Most foals are born at night.

When it is time to give **birth**, the mother horse finds somewhere safe to lie down. Sometimes, she gives birth by herself. Other times, farmers may need to help get her foal out.

9

FANTASTIC FOALS

When the foal is born, its mother licks it all over. This cleans the baby horse. It will be able to stand and walk soon after.

Foals learn their mother's scent a few days after they are born.

10

Newborn horses are very big babies. Some can weigh about 100 pounds (45 kg). That is about the same weight as a tire from a large truck.

11

MOTHER'S MILK

A foal drinks milk from its mother's body about two hours after it is born. This milk gives the baby the **nutrients** it needs to have a healthy start to life.

Foals grow quickly! They can gain about 3 lbs. (1 kg) each day.

12

Within a couple of weeks, the baby horse starts nibbling on hay along with drinking milk. After a few months, the foal switches to eating only solid foods.

13

YEARLINGS

Young female horses are called fillies, and **males** are called colts. When the horses are about a year old, they are called yearlings.

14

Yearlings look like small adult horses.

Yearlings play together. This helps build their **communication** skills. The young horses may run and chase one another. Sometimes, farmers give them large balls to play with.

15

ALL GROWN UP

Horses are considered adults when they are about five years old. As adults, many horses are able to **mate** and have their own foals. However, farmers sometimes make it so some males are unable to mate. Those horses are called geldings.

Geldings are used to do work rather than mate.

16

Many adult horses are trained to do work on farms. They often pull heavy equipment through fields. Some farmers ride horses while rounding up other farm animals.

STALLIONS AND MARES

Adult female horses are called mares. Adult males that can mate are stallions. They are usually bigger than mares. A stallion can weigh more than 2,000 lbs. (900 kg).

MARE

STALLION

MANE

Mares usually have thinner manes than stallions.

Most mares have their first foal when they are about five years old. Many continue having babies until they are about 15 years old.

THE END OF LIFE

Horses don't have many **predators**. But they do need to look out for bears, wolves, and cougars. Farmers bring horses into barns at night to keep them safe.

A COUGAR

A WOLF

A BEAR

Veterinarians are people who take care of the health of animals.

Horses can live for about 30 years. Some horses may live longer if they are fed well and have regular checkups.

21

LIFE CYCLE
OF A HORSE

A horse begins its life as a foal. The foal drinks milk from its mother and grows into a yearling. The yearling continues to grow and becomes an adult.

YEARLING

FOAL

ADULT HORSE

During its life, a horse may have foals of its own. Eventually, the horse will die, but the foals live on and have even more horses. This keeps the life cycle going!

Glossary

birth when a female has a baby

communication the sharing of information

domestic tamed for use by humans

female a horse that can give birth to young

livestock animals that are raised by people on farms or ranches

males horses that cannot give birth to young

mate to come together to produce young

nutrients substances needed by animals to grow and stay healthy

predators animals that hunt and eat other animals

pregnant when a female animal has babies growing inside her

Index